A Planet Is a Poem

Written by
Amanda West Lewis

Illustrated by
Oliver Averill

Kids Can Press

For Morris and Mae — A.W.L.

For my son, Oscar, and my partner Molly. I hope you enjoy the book. — O.A.

ACKNOWLEDGMENTS

This book owes much to the keen editorial eye of Kathleen Keenan. It was a far bigger challenge than either of us realized, and she did an amazing job in helping me to pull it all together. Thank you, Kathleen! Oliver Averill has done an amazing job of bringing my poetry and our solar system alive through his vibrant illustrations. Thank you so much, Oliver! Most of the solar system research for this book was gleaned from the NASA Solar System website: https://solarsystem.nasa.gov/. I highly recommend this site for any burgeoning planetary scientists. I am enormously grateful to Jacob Berkowitz for his expertise and his reading of the manuscript for clarity and scientific accuracy. Any factual errors are entirely my own. Mary Quattlebaum and the VCFA PB Jebbies encouraged me into the concept of the book. Shelley Nosbisch helped with resources for hip-hop poetry, and Alexander Wynne-Jones worked with me on the poem "Your Turn." Thank you to designer Marie Bartholomew, who collaborated on the creation of the concrete poem "Jupiter the Giant." I am continually humbled by the wisdom and gentle advice I receive from Tim Wynne-Jones, who helps to unlock the poetry in my heart.

Published in Canada and the U.S. by Kids Can Press Ltd.
25 Dockside Drive, Toronto, ON M5A 0B5

Kids Can Press is a Corus Entertainment Inc. company

www.kidscanpress.com

The artwork in this book was rendered in Photoshop and Procreate.
The text is set in Grandstander.

Edited by Kathleen Keenan
Designed by Marie Bartholomew

Printed and bound in Shenzhen, China, in 10/2023 by C & C Offset

MIX
Paper | Supporting responsible forestry
FSC® C008047

CM 24 0 9 8 7 6 5 4 3 2 1

Library and Archives Canada Cataloguing in Publication

Title: A planet is a poem / written by Amanda West Lewis ; illustrated by Oliver Averill.
Names: Lewis, Amanda West, author. | Averill, Oliver, illustrator.
Identifiers: Canadiana (print) 20230220908 | Canadiana (ebook) 20230221653 | ISBN 9781525304422 (hardcover) | ISBN 9781525304729 (EPUB)
Subjects: LCSH: Solar system — Juvenile poetry. | LCGFT: Poetry.
Classification: LCC QB501.4 .L49 2024 | DDC j523.2 — dc23

Kids Can Press gratefully acknowledges that the land on which our office is located is the traditional territory of many nations, including the Mississaugas of the Credit, the Anishnabeg, the Chippewa, the Haudenosaunee and the Wendat peoples, and is now home to many diverse First Nations, Inuit and Métis peoples.

We thank the Government of Ontario, through Ontario Creates and the Ontario Arts Council; the Canada Council for the Arts; and the Government of Canada for their financial support of our publishing activity.

Canada Council for the Arts
Conseil des arts du Canada

ONTARIO ARTS COUNCIL
CONSEIL DES ARTS DE L'ONTARIO
an Ontario government agency
un organisme du gouvernement de l'Ontario

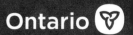
Ontario

Contents

A Planet Is a Poem

We know more about space than ever before. With new, powerful telescopes, computers and cameras, scientists are discovering that the solar system is even more surprising, miraculous, bizarre and poetic than we thought.

Poetic? Actually, planetary scientists — the people who study the planets, satellites and other bodies in our solar system — are some of the most poetic people around! They need to describe our solar system, but what they've discovered is so incredible, it's almost impossible to find the words. So, they try to capture your imagination using images and metaphors.

Poets do that, too. Every poem is its own world filled with images, sounds and rhythms.

A planet is a poem. A poem is a planet.

A Poem Is a Planet

Poems play with sounds and rhythms. Your life is filled with rhythm, starting with the rhythm of your heartbeat: da-**dum**, da-**dum**, da-**dum**. The words you speak every day have sounds just like that, stressed and unstressed sounds like the sound of your heartbeat.

The word **heart**beat is **stressed**/unstressed: **dum**-da.

To**day** is unstressed/**stressed**: da-**dum**.

So is bi**zarre**: da-**dum**.

And **so**lar **sys**tem is **dum**-da **dum**-da.

Try saying "a poem is a planet" and see which syllables you emphasize. See if you can find the beat of the unstressed and stressed syllables.

In English, there are names for those beats. An unstressed sound followed by a stressed sound is called an iamb (pronounced "I am"). There are other beat patterns, but because iambs are like heartbeats, poets use them a lot.

Some poems use iambs in particular patterns. For example, a line with five iambs is called an iambic pentameter (*penta* means "five"). But poetry doesn't always have to follow the rules. Sometimes writers cheat a little! William Shakespeare would use an apostrophe to leave out a syllable. Let your voice glide over the missing sound:

I **do** for**give** thy **robb**'ry, **gen**tle **thief.**

How a poem *looks* is also important. Some poems group lines together, some put lines or words in patterns. A group of lines in a poem is called a stanza or a verse. Stanzas and the way that lines are put on the page can be clues to figuring out the world of the poem.

In our solar system, each planet has its own rhythm, depending on its orbit, its spin and its distance from the sun. Each poem in this collection has its own rhythm, too. You can look for clues about each planet by finding the rhythm, rhyme and sounds that the poems make. But these planets and poems are just a start. There are billions of undiscovered planets in our galaxy — maybe you'll find your own beats and sounds to write poems for new planets!

Our Family
A Sonnet for the Solar System

A cloud of gas contracts into a disk.
It spins and swirls, ignites and makes a star.
Now dust and gas both smash and crash, they whisk,
Collide and stick, the bits twirl near and far.
Some huge, they form eight planets smooth and round.
Now we look up amazed when day is done —
What's there to see? What's to be found?
We're awed by things that circle 'round our sun.
We marvel, study, watch and find much more,
As ast'roids, planets, comets, rocks and rings —
All move, like Earth, around the sun, our core.
A swirling sky of countless moving things!
A family made of many complex parts,
Our solar system's great adventure starts.

WE'RE ALL SPINNING AROUND THE SUN!

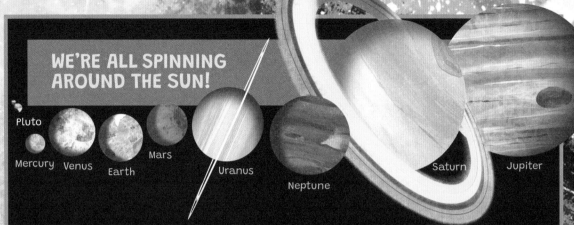

Pluto

Mercury   Venus

Earth

Mars

Uranus

Neptune

Saturn   Jupiter

Our solar system was formed about 4.5 billion years ago when a giant, rotating cloud of gas and dust — a solar nebula — spun until it collapsed and flattened into a disk. Most of the gas and dust was pulled into the center of the disk, igniting to form a star — our sun. What was left over from the disk formed everything else in our solar system: the planets, dwarf planets, asteroids and comets.

Today, we count eight planets and five dwarf planets in our solar system. Beyond the planet Neptune is a huge area called the Kuiper Belt, where thousands of comets and billions of asteroids circle the sun. And beyond the Kuiper Belt may be the Oort cloud, an area planetary scientists think of as a thick-walled shell, a kind of bubble made of icy, comet-like pieces — but they're not sure if it's even there! With new telescopes and space probes, we are finding out that the solar system is stranger and more wonderful than we ever imagined.

Sonnets Sing

The word *sonnet* means
"little song." Sonnets were made famous
by William Shakespeare. Most sonnets have
14 lines and focus on one idea with a change,
or "turn," at the end. Every other line of a
sonnet usually rhymes, except the last two,
which rhyme with each other. Those two
are called a rhyming couplet.

This sonnet uses five stressed beats in each
line. It's filled with heartbeats! I cheated a
bit on the word *ast'roid*, which is actually
asteroid. (Remember, poetry doesn't
always follow the rules!)

O Sol! O Helios!
An Ode to the Sun

I

O Sol! O Helios! Our sun!
Shining for billions of years.
Your core is a constant and fiery explosion
That never disappears.

Your particles spin into space, your solar winds flow
And race throughout the sky. Your rays stream,
Magnetic poles switch and reverse, your flares flash bright —
With spots and storms you are a dynamo!
On Earth our power source is your bright beam.
At night your vibrant sunsets are supreme,
We wake to sing and praise your golden light.

II

O Sun! Our Star! To us you're special.
Without you there's no life on Earth.
Your heat and light to us are central.
We orbit around your girth.

At night we count the stars we see by billions,
Lighting up our milky galaxy.
Infinite in numbers past our sight,
A universe of stars — there must be zillions!
Some old, some young, they all spin distantly,
And most with planets held by gravity,
Although to us they're only sparks of light.

III

O Sol! Our Star! This fact is true,
Unique to us, no question:
There's life on Earth because of you.
This ode's for you, O Sun!

You also circle 'round the galaxy
In motion slow you hold us in our place,
Where there are other stars all spinning, too,
But you are special to the life we see.
Although there may be more like you in space
It's you who is uniquely Earth's birthplace.
O Sol, our sun, you shine and dazzle true.

Honoring Odes

An ode is a poem that praises something.
Odes usually have three sections. The first
starts a theme, praising the subject. The second
section presents another point of view. The third
section brings the two viewpoints together.

Some odes have a very particular rhythm and
rhyme scheme. This ode is modeled on a poem
called "To Autumn" by John Keats. The first
stanza alternates between four beats and
three beats in each line. The second stanza
uses five stressed beats in each line. See
if you can figure out the pattern in
the rhyming words at the end of
the lines.

OUR SPECTACULAR SUN!

Our sun is a medium-sized yellow dwarf star — but 1.3 million Earths could fit inside it! It's made mostly of hydrogen. Deep in the sun's core, where it's 15 million degrees C (27 million degrees F), hydrogen is constantly being squished and changed into helium. This process releases heat and light. The light particles (photons) made in the sun's core take 170 000 years to reach the surface, but then they fly out in all directions at 290 000 km (180 000 mi.) per hour! Those zooming, electrically charged particles emit deadly radiation. Thankfully, Earth's atmosphere protects us.

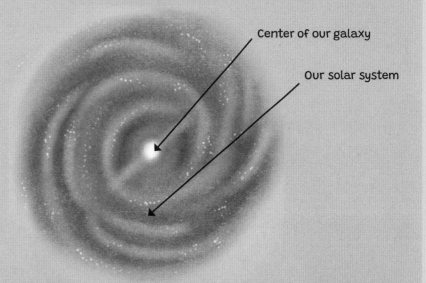

Center of our galaxy

Our solar system

As we orbit around the sun, the sun itself is on its own long orbit around the center of our galaxy. It takes the sun 230 million years to make one complete circuit!

Scientists believe that our sun is halfway through its life cycle and will eventually burn itself out. When it has no more hydrogen to convert to helium, it will cool down and stop spinning. All the planets, dwarf planets, asteroids and comets in our solar system will then crash into the sun as it dies. But don't worry — that won't happen for at least 4.5 billion years!

A Planet of Craters Creative
Rhyming Beats for Mercury

Mercury's tiny —
Of planets, the smallest.
But named for a god
Who was known as the fastest.

Just eighty-eight days
To circle the sun.
Of all of the planets
There's no faster one —

And yet it spins slowly!
One Mercury day
Will see fifty-five
Earth days turn away.

So close to the sun
Makes daytime too hot.
With no trees or shade
You'd melt on the spot.

With no atmosphere
To hold in that heat,
The nights are quite frigid
They'd freeze off your feet!

Cliffs a mile high.
A crust made of rock.
A core made of lava.
A surface that's pocked.

Meteors slammed
The surface and made
Some four hundred craters —
Rocks flew out and sprayed.

These bits of crushed rock
Reflect the sun's rays.
They sparkle and shimmer,
They're called crater rays.

There's one special crater
Where rocks are profuse,
The special-est of craters
It's named *Dr. Seuss*!

Bouncing Beats and Rhythmic Rhymes

This poem uses two beats in each line and catchy, strong rhymes. A small, fast beat helps you feel how small, fast Mercury whizzes around the sun. You've probably read other poems that do this, maybe by writers like Dennis Lee, Shel Silverstein or Dr. Seuss. It's a common poetic technique because you can tell a story with few words, yet the rhymes and beats make it bounce off the page and stick in your mind.

FAST-FOOTED MERCURY

The Roman god Mercury was a messenger for the other gods, so it makes sense that our fastest-orbiting planet is named after him. Mercury is closest to the sun and is the smallest planet in our solar system, only a little bit bigger than our moon. Like Earth, Venus and Mars, it is a terrestrial planet, meaning it has a rocky crust around a central, molten core of lava.

If you were on Mercury's surface, the sun would look three times larger and seven times brighter than it does from Earth. Of course, with daytime temperatures of 430°C (806°F), nighttime temperatures of −180°C (−292°F), no air to breathe and constant bombardment by solar plasma, you wouldn't last very long!

We've named the craters on Mercury to honor Earth's artists, musicians, writers and dancers. There are craters for Shakespeare, Picasso and, yes, Dr. Seuss!

Our Sister Planet
A Villanelle for Venus

Venus spins slowly, the opposite way,
Earth-like in size, air hazy with sulfur.
The bright light we see at the start of the day.

Her sky is deep orange, her rocks are dark gray,
Volcanoes pour lava on mountains and craters.
Venus spins slowly the opposite way.

Covered in clouds that reflect the sun's rays,
Storm-lightning flashes through, layer on layer.
The bright light we see at the end of the day.

Sunrise in the west, months pass in one day.
Her axis is straight — no seasons to savor.
Venus spins slowly the opposite way.

Carbon dioxide traps heat and it stays —
In our solar system there's no planet hotter.
The bright light we see at the start of the day.

With our sister planet we dance a ballet,
Perfect paired partners, two dancers that differ.
Venus spins slowly, the opposite way,
The bright light we see at the end of the day.
The bright light we see at the start of the day.

VENUS THE BRIGHT LIGHT

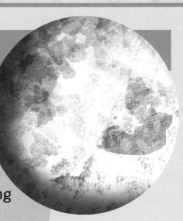

Venus is Earth's closest neighbor, almost identical in size and structure with an intensely hot iron core covered by a mantle of churning molten rock. Both planets have thin rock crusts that bulge and move, creating volcanoes as the mantle shifts below.

But there are some important differences. Venus has a thick atmosphere of carbon dioxide and sulfuric acid. This traps heat and makes Venus the hottest planet in our solar system, with surface temperatures of 465°C (900°F).

Venus spins in the opposite direction to Earth. There, the sun rises in the west and sets in the east. One day on Venus is the equivalent of 225 Earth days! It also spins straight up and down, but Earth spins on a tilted axis, which creates seasons when different parts of the planet move closer or farther from the sun. With hardly any tilt, Venus has no seasons.

The clouds on Venus reflect sunlight, and Venus can often be seen shining on our horizon at twilight or first thing in the morning, as the sun is rising.

Variable Villanelle

A villanelle has six stanzas of three lines. The first and third lines of each stanza rhyme. They also repeat as alternating last lines in each verse before meeting up at the end. This pattern shows two different ideas gradually coming together, just like how Venus and Earth have similarities and differences that keep them apart, but also bind them together.

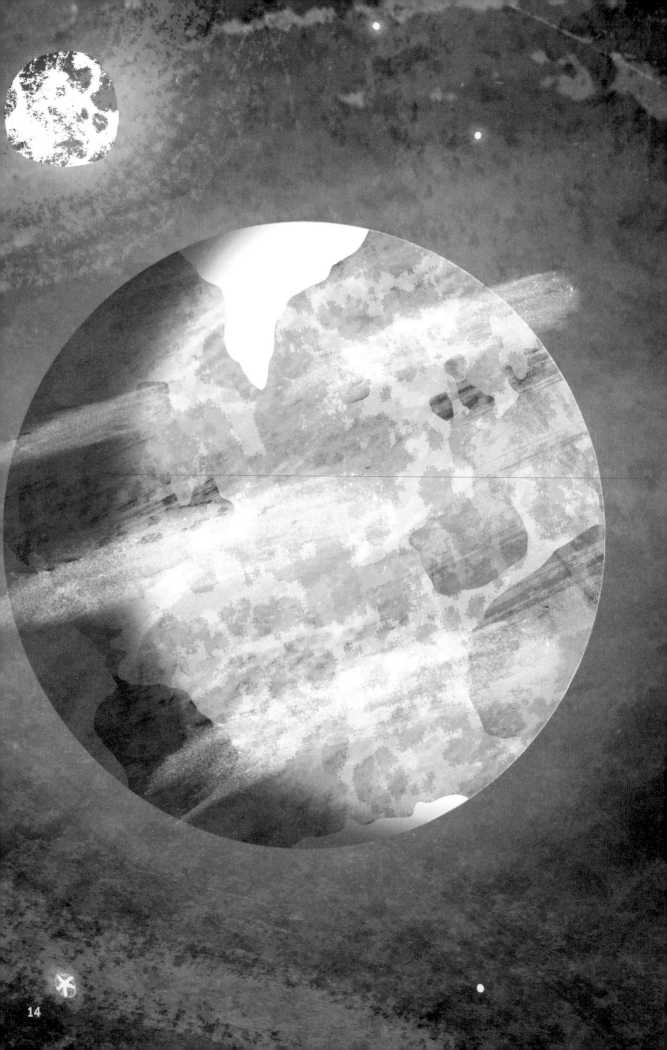

Only One Home
A Ballad of Earth

Our Earth is unique, as far as we know
    We're in a sweet spot near the sun.
A "Goldilocks" rock, not too hot, not too cold,
    Just right for us all to live on.

Our planet is lush because there is soil
    That grows food to feed everyone.
On Earth we have mountains and canyons and trees
    A planet with people? Just one!

Our atmosphere's precious, perfect for breath —
    An oxygen-nitrogen stew.
The nitrogen molecules scatter sun's light
    Making our sky look bright blue.

When planets were formed, they whizzed all around
    And some crashed into each other
One planet hit Earth and bits flew right off —
    Our moon is discarded Earth matter!

But maybe the most important of all:
    There's water on Earth, that is clear.
Water is life, it's where we come from,
    Without it we wouldn't be here.

With Earth as our home, we can study and learn,
    Name things, explore, climb a tree.
All thought that exists is because of our home
    Unique among all — planet three.

So let's raise a cheer for the Earth, for our home,
    Agree to protect this thin crust,
There's only one planet that's perfect for us —
    Without it we're just cosmic dust!

Dancing Ballads:

The word *ballad* comes from the
Italian word *ballare*, meaning "to dance"
(as in "ballet"). Ballads usually have four lines
in each verse, with every other line rhyming. The
lines alternate between four stressed beats
and three stressed beats.

A ballad is a poem that is like a song,
spoken or sung to a crowd of people, to tell
a story. Scientists think that humans have
been singing songs for about half a million
years, so a ballad seems the right
form to tell the story
of our home.

OUR EARTH. OUR HOME.

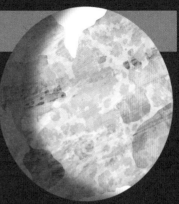

We've called our planet "Earth" for more than a thousand years. The word is a blend of Old English and German words that mean "ground." In Latin, the word was *terra* (think "terrestrial" and "extraterrestrial").

Earth is the fifth-largest planet in our solar system, the third from the sun and the largest terrestrial planet. It's made up of four layers:

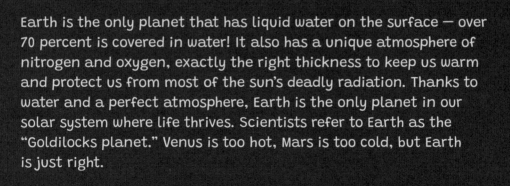

a core of hot, solid iron and nickel at 5400°C (9800°F)

a layer of liquid iron and nickel

a mantle of molten hot, flowing rock, 2900 km (1800 mi.) thick

the outer crust, only 30 km (19 mi.) thick, but constantly changing and growing

Earth is the only planet that has liquid water on the surface — over 70 percent is covered in water! It also has a unique atmosphere of nitrogen and oxygen, exactly the right thickness to keep us warm and protect us from most of the sun's deadly radiation. Thanks to water and a perfect atmosphere, Earth is the only planet in our solar system where life thrives. Scientists refer to Earth as the "Goldilocks planet." Venus is too hot, Mars is too cold, but Earth is just right.

I'm Just Me
Mars Talks Back

They gave me the name of their god of war
Because I appear as blood red
They made me their excuse to fight battles
But I'm not like that
I'm just me

They saw there were lines, spider tracks on the ground
Cracks that were caused by dried rain
They said those were roads to civilizations
But there are no roads
That's just me

They sent up space probes to poke and to prod me
Found nothing that they thought important
They took away rocks and left tons of junk
But I'm not a junkyard
I'm me

Long ago, I had rain pour in torrents
Long ago, I had air they could breathe
Long ago, I had rivers and lakes
Long ago, I was lush blue and green

Now I am dry, with huge winds and seasons
My year's twice as long, there's some gravity
They say: "Close enough, red Mars could be home!"
But there's much they don't know
About me

They've sent up some rovers and flown a small drone
Collected some rocks and debris
They're looking for clues to what's in my past
But do they understand what they see?
I'm so much more
I am me!

Up Close
and Personal

This poem is written as though Mars
were talking to you. It's called a mask or
persona poem. Taking an object and giving
it a voice like this is called "personification."
Personification isn't only a style in poetry, you
can use it for all kinds of writing. Try writing
a story in the voice of a drone abandoned
on the surface of Mars or in the voice of
a spaceship returning to Earth.
You'll see things from a whole
new perspective!

MARS, PLANET OF STORIES

Mars is named after the Roman god of war. The Romans used to watch the way Mars moved in the sky to decide if they should go to war. Earth and Mars are very similar geographically, with volcanoes, canyons and impact craters, as well as polar ice caps. Both are slightly tilted on an axis and have seasons. Our days are almost the same length.

But there are many differences. While Earth looks blue because of water, Mars has no liquid water and looks red, thanks to the iron-rich dust flying through its atmosphere. Mars has two moons, and a Martian year is almost twice as long as ours. It is much colder there: −63°C (−81°F) in the daytime. And the thin Martian atmosphere is mostly carbon dioxide, with hardly any oxygen.

Even with these differences, Mars seems inviting. Humans have always been fascinated by the "Red Planet" and we've sent up a number of probes to learn more. Some scientists are working hard to find a way for humans to travel there. Who knows? Maybe one day, you'll go there and find out things for yourself!

Jupiter the Giant
Concrete Poem for Jupiter

PLANET-SIZED CYCLONES.
ANTI-Cyclones. Polar storm. ANTI-CYCLONES.
CLOUDS OF AMMONIA AND WATER CHURN, WHIRL, WHISK INTO STORMS
AN ATMOSPHERE OF HYDROGEN AND HELIUM LIKE A STAR !CYCLONES!
MADE of twice as much stuff as all other planets COMBINED.
IT'S MASSIVE! ALMOST A STAR! A STAR THAT DIDN'T IGNITE.
SEVENTY-nine moons orbit, like planets in their own solar system. A huge MAGNET.
SPINNING FAST, INCREDIBLY FAST! !WHOOSH! STIRRING THE ATMOSPHERE
INTO LIGHT AND DARK STRIPES. SPINNING MAKES BELTS AND ZONES, MAKES
VIOLENT, TERRIFYING STORMS. THICK BLANKETS OF
SWIRLING CLOUDS, SWIRLING BELTS. FEROCIOUS
GALES. FIERCE BLASTS. A ROARING STORM AS BIG
AS EARTH. THE GIANT RED SPOT. THE GIANT RED SPOT SPOT.
HUNDREDS OF EARTH YEARS OLD. IS SHRINKING, RAGING.
RAGING HOWLING. THIN RINGS ABOVE. TEARING OFF, VANISHING, BELOW,
INTO SPINNING CLOUDS. SOUP,
NO SOLID GROUND. A SEARING, BURNING
THE LARGEST OCEAN IN THE SOLAR SYSTEM.
AN OCEAN OF LIQUID NITROGEN, SUPER-HOT, DENSE.
MASSIVE CRUSHING PRESSURE. THE WEIGHT
OF FIFTY THOUSAND ELEPHANTS ON EVERY INCH OF YOUR BODY
ALMOST a star. It didn't ignite. Seventy-nine moons orbit, like a SOLAR
SYSTEM. More stuff than all the other planets combined. MOLECULES,
GASSES, chemicals. Swirling. Spinning incredibly FAST.
PLANET-sized Cyclones. Polar storm. Planet-sized CYCLONES.
PLANET-SIZED CYCLONES.

JUPITER THE KING

Named after the Roman king of the gods, Jupiter really is the king of our planets. Not only is it larger than the other planets combined, but scientists now think that Jupiter may have created Earth!

When our solar system was forming, Jupiter was much closer to the sun, about where Mars is now. Scientists think that there were other big planets there, too. But massive Jupiter spins quickly, creating a powerful gravitational pull so strong that it made other planets smash into one another. Some of the bits and pieces, or space stuff (scientists love the word *stuff*), fell into the sun, and some stuck together to create Mercury, Venus, Mars and Earth. It may be that Jupiter really is Earth's parent!

So far, planetary scientists have discovered 79 moons orbiting Jupiter. The four largest are the size of small planets! All 79 orbit around Jupiter as though it were a sun — which it almost is. Jupiter is very hot inside, about 24 000°C (43 000°F). If it were a bit hotter, its gasses would have ignited into flame. It would have been a small star, the center of its own solar system.

Europa

Ganymede

Lo

Callisto

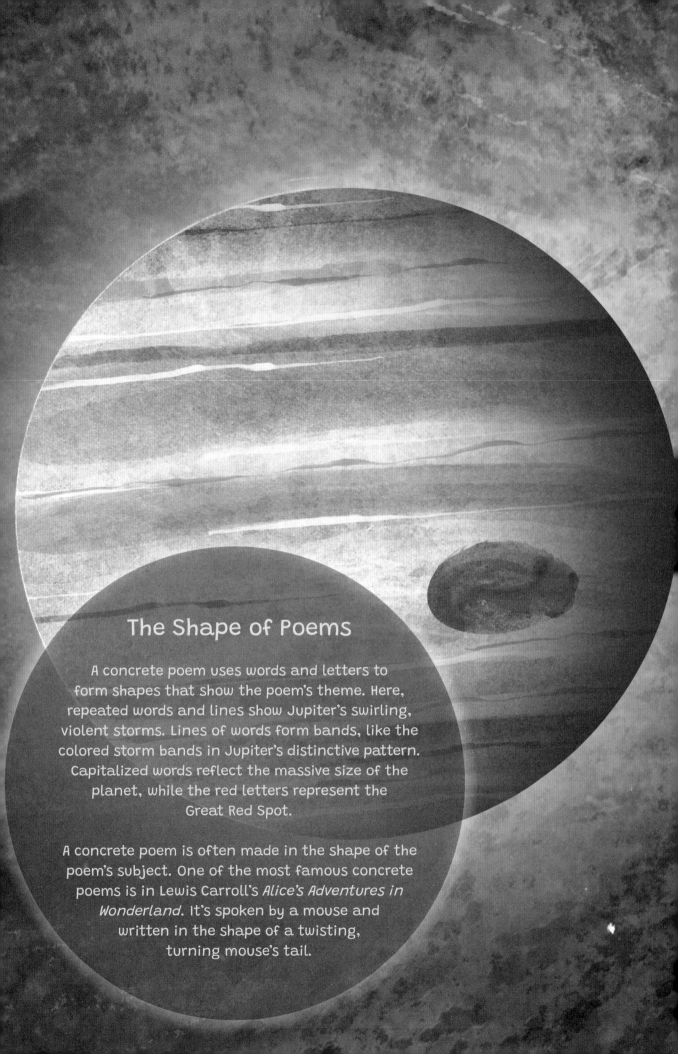

The Shape of Poems

A concrete poem uses words and letters to form shapes that show the poem's theme. Here, repeated words and lines show Jupiter's swirling, violent storms. Lines of words form bands, like the colored storm bands in Jupiter's distinctive pattern. Capitalized words reflect the massive size of the planet, while the red letters represent the Great Red Spot.

A concrete poem is often made in the shape of the poem's subject. One of the most famous concrete poems is in Lewis Carroll's *Alice's Adventures in Wonderland*. It's spoken by a mouse and written in the shape of a twisting, turning mouse's tail.

A Puzzle of Sixes
Saturn's Spinning Sestina

The surface of Saturn's not solid like Earth.
Helium, hydrogen, more gasses spinning,
Making bold stripes, both dark and light.
But Saturn is famous because of its rings
Formed from small rocks and chunks of ice
Smashed by collisions with asteroids and moons.

Around Saturn orbit eighty-two moons.
Hard to see from far-away Earth.
One called Enceladus is coated in ice.
Water sprays from its crust while it's spinning,
And some of that spray creates one of the rings.
The rest falls like snow that shines in the light.

Enceladus snows and reflects the sun's light,
It's unique and the brightest of moons.
Titan's the largest of moons in the rings,
With a thick atmosphere as we have on Earth.
Moons called "The Shepherds" are always there, spinning,
Their gravity gathering free-floating ice.

There's red dust mixed in, combined with the ice,
It shimmers and shines, reflects in Sun's light.
A six-sided jet stream is caused by the spinning
Of Saturn's unusual, beautiful rings.
We're solving the puzzle, we're watching from Earth,
Searching for beauty in jet streams and moons.

Saturn has mystery past all the rings.
It's cold, but maybe there's life in the ice
(We know there is life in the deep ice on Earth.)
The seasons on Saturn shift dark blue to light,
And what might we find on her many strange moons
The size of small planets all orbiting, spinning?

Everything's held by the force of the spinning,
Rotation and gravity hold Saturn's rings.
The spin streaks the jet streams, the spin guides the moons,
The spin makes Enceladus form tides of ice.
It's cold and it's dark, far from the sun's light,
Yet Saturn has seasons that change, like on Earth.

Exceptional moons and gas storms all spinning —
Down here on Earth we can see Saturn's rings,
A poem of ice that shines in the light.

STUNNINGLY BEAUTIFUL SATURN

Saturn is the second-largest planet in our solar system — you could fit nine Earths across the middle! It may have as many as 82 moons and some help to shape and sculpt the rings. These are called shepherd moons. Saturn isn't the only planet with rings, but it does have the largest, most noticeable rings. They're made of pieces of asteroids, comets and moons that collided and smashed when Saturn was formed. The strong gravitational pull formed them into thousands of ringlets. They aren't very tall, only about three times your height, but from Earth, they look like seven distinct rings.

Saturn is tilted on its axis, and so, like Earth, it has seasons, but each season lasts seven Earth years. During Saturn's summer, it looks golden, but in winter, it looks blue. That's because it's so cold that all the clouds sink, and more blue light scatters in the atmosphere.

Saturn spins almost as fast as Jupiter — one day on Saturn is only 10.7 Earth hours long. Because it's so large and spins so quickly, it has incredibly powerful jet streams, storms and gas-cloud winds. There's an amazing, unique six-sided jet stream at Saturn's north pole that is 30 000 km (19 000 mi.) across, with a massive rotating storm in the middle.

A Sestina Puzzle

A sestina is a puzzle of sixes:
six words are repeated at the end of
six stanzas of six lines each. They're all
repeated in the last three lines, too. Can
you find the six puzzle words in this poem?
Can you figure out the pattern? Try tracing
each of the words with your finger as you
read. The result is repeated, spinning words
that move through the whole poem like
the rings of a spiral. And since Saturn
has a unique six-sided jet stream, it
deserves a unique puzzle
poem of sixes!

Rolling Sideways
A Free Verse Poem for Uranus

Uranus is a free spirit
    Rolling round the distant sun
        Spinning like Venus, opposite,
        And sideways
        Like a barrel
        (Not a top).

The magnetic field's wonky.
    Because of its spin
        it stretches away as a magnetic tail.
        Swooshing and pulling,
           corkscrewing off.
                Millions of miles of magnetic force
              Trails free Uranus
                in space.

Made of gas, like Jupiter and Saturn —
An Ice Giant.
    Coldest of all.
        Winds and storms we can't see
           Under a frozen, methane-blue haze
           Mixed with hydrogen sulfide.

Thirteen thin rings spin, down and up.
Tiny bits of dust and rock
        Scatter blue light —
        Make blue rings.

Twenty-seven moons orbit, up and down with the rings.
Shepherd moons sculpt the rings,
    Keep them thin,
        Hold them in place.
        A sideways halo.
    A moon called Miranda's a Frankenstein moon —
Pieced together with parts that don't fit.

Charged particles fresh from the sun
        Caught up by magnetic fields
           Sparkle and crackle.

        A light show.
        Auroras.
        High above methane clouds.
        Sideways magic.

Freedom
in Free Verse

✦

Free verse poetry doesn't have a
special pattern or use beats, although
there is usually a sense of rhythm. Free
verse doesn't have to rhyme. It's more
like the way people speak, but the words
are carefully chosen for how they look
or sound. In a free verse poem, how
a line breaks can help emphasize the
meaning or theme of the poem. Free
verse seemed the perfect choice for
a planet that spins sideways
in its own unique way!

URANUS, THE SIDEWAYS PLANET

Uranus is unique in our solar system because of the way it spins sideways like a barrel. Scientists think that a huge rock, about the size of Earth, hit Uranus billions of years ago and knocked it sideways, where it has remained ever since.

On Earth, the magnetosphere (the magnetic field that a planet creates by spinning) runs north and south in about the same place as the geographic poles. But on Uranus, the magnets don't line up with the sideways poles. Because of this and its sideways rotation, the planet's magnetic field twists off into the solar system, pulling in bits of debris for millions of miles.

In 1986, the space probe Voyager 2 flew past Uranus, and we learned that Uranus has rings, just like Saturn. The rings spin around its middle, but because of the sideways tilt, they appear to run up and down. The probe also showed that Uranus has many more moons than scientists originally thought. So far, we've counted 27 and named them for characters in plays and poems. So, Uranus is the most literary planet!

What's in a Name?

An Acrostic Poem for Neptune

Neptune seems a brilliant blue ball —
Except beneath calm gas clouds,
Powerful storms rage, while roiling, boiling liquid gas churns.
Terrifying lightning flashes constantly.
Under such pressure, the atmosphere could rain diamonds!
No other planet has such violent storms.
Extremes write the story of fierce Neptune.

Across the Lines

Acrostics are fun puzzle
poems where the first letter of each
line spells out a word, name or a phrase
when read vertically. Neptune was named
after the Roman god of the sea. For many
years, we thought it was a smooth, calm ball.
But now we know that it is a planet of fierce
extremes and contradictions. So, while its name
is familiar, we are finding out new things about
what lies under those clouds every day. It's
like an acrostic where we know the name,
but each poem line tells us something
about what lies beyond that name.
Try making an acrostic with your
name, writing something about
yourself on each line.

INVISIBLE NEPTUNE

Astronomers didn't know about Neptune until 1846, when a scientist used math and the orbits of other planets to predict that it existed, even though no one had seen it.

Like Uranus, Neptune is an ice giant, as wide as four Earths side by side. We've never sent a probe to Neptune, but with powerful telescopes and probes flying nearby, we've seen the rings and arcs, and found Neptune's 14 moons. Triton might have started out as a dwarf planet like Pluto and been pulled from deep outer space by Neptune's gravity. It orbits Neptune in the opposite direction of the other moons and has a lumpy, cantaloupe-textured crust created by errupting frozen lava and geysers.

Triton

Neptune is a planet of extremes. Hot, cold. Gas, ice. A Neptune day is only 16 hours long (one of the solar system's shortest days), but it takes 165 Earth years to orbit around the sun (one of the longest years). Neptune's seasons each last about 40 years!

Under Neptune's calm outer clouds swirls an atmosphere of highly pressurized methane, helium and hydrogen gasses. Frozen white methane gets whipped up and bursts through the blue gas clouds — making a smell like rotten eggs! The extreme pressure in the gas clouds could turn carbon atoms into diamonds — imagine diamonds raining down through the clouds!

Paired Dwarves
Pluto and Charon, Poetic Companions

Four million miles away from the sun,
Two bodies spinning together as one.

> Our knowledge of Charon has only begun.

The tiny dwarf Pluto is circl'ing around
In tandem with Charon — together they're bound.

> Charon's much more than a moon, we've found.

Facing each other, they spin in a dance
Partners together — a strange circumstance.

> We look at the pictures and see at a glance

In our solar system these two are unique,
Their landscapes dramatic, not dull, not bleak

> A moat with a mountain, an Everest-high peak.

Marvels we've seen, amazing and true,
The skies above Pluto, like Earth's, are bright blue!

> Pluto sees Charon always in view.

Frosty volcanoes spew nitrogen mud,
Ice mountains appear the color of blood

> With geysers of ice that are too cold to flood

With strong solar winds that constantly blow
The atmosphere freezes then falls as red snow.

> From Pluto to Charon the red gasses flow.

We see a plateau that's shaped like a heart
The winds make it sift — a huge work of art.

> Neither Charon nor Pluto could manage apart

Pluto depends on the tiny dwarf Charon.
They stay close together, their destinies sharing.

> Two peaceful co-planets, a perfect space pairing.

OUR FAVORITE DWARF PLANET

Dwarf planets are not called that because of their size. Dwarf planets have strange, irregular orbits that make them swerve into other planets' orbits. But Pluto *is* small — about half the width of the United States.

Pluto's unusual, oval-shaped orbit means it is sometimes close to the sun and sometimes far, far away. When it is close, Pluto's frozen molecules of water, nitrogen and methane thaw. Then, when it's farther away, the gasses refreeze to fall back to the surface as red snow. In fact, color is a big feature of Pluto's landscape. There's a huge reddish heart shape as big as Texas (called Tombaugh Regio) that was carved out by an ancient glacier. And the distant sun lights up tiny particles in the atmosphere, turning Pluto's sky a beautiful shade of blue.

Charon is unique, too: it has a "mountain in a moat," taller than Mount Everest, sitting below the surface with just the peak sticking out. Scientists used to call Charon a moon, but now they aren't so sure. It's about half Pluto's size and 20 times closer to Pluto than our moon is to us. Pluto and Charon orbit around a shared gravitational center. Scientists think they might be co-planets — they need each other to stay in their 248-year orbit around the sun.

Poem Companions

These poems are two separate poems
that can be combined into one to make a
companion poem. Since Pluto is twice the size
of Charon, the poem for Pluto is twice the size.
Both poems are written in tetrameters, which
means there are four stressed beats in each
line. Pluto's poem is written in rhyming
couplets, and when combined, the two
poems form rhyming triplets.

The way these two poems fit together
is similar to how Pluto and Charon work
together to stay in orbit around the
sun, even though they are
separate objects.

Not a Belt
A Prose Poem for the Kuiper Belt

Not a belt, but a fat donut. A donut coated with trillions of sprinkles — bits of rock, ice and dust, odds and ends from the birth of the solar system. Glitters in the sky. Images in the sky. A tiny pancake. A snowman. A mysterious X.

Not a belt, but a dance with the two giants, Jupiter and Neptune, dancing at the side, throwing their gravity around, pushing and pulling, making the space stuff beyond them swirl. They toss smaller dancers — tiny dwarf planets, rings and moons — spin them in and out. Dancing pairs of ice and rock tango, sticking together to form new shapes.

Not a belt, but a stormy sea, blown by solar winds. Specks of ice, rock, leftover stuff from the beginning of time sparkle in the sun, scattered on the waves. Bright comets stream long tails through the cosmic ocean.

But it is a belt, too. Our chubby solar system bulges beyond Neptune. The belt holds it in, holds trillions of bits and bites in motion around the sun. Rocks, comets, planets and dust all dance, a belted donut salsa on stormy seas.

What Makes It a Poem?

This poem is called a prose poem. It's written out like regular prose in short paragraphs. But a prose poem plays with the sounds and meanings of words. A prose poem is filled with images and metaphors that create new meanings. Saying that the Kuiper Belt is a donut is a metaphor. Describing a binary planetesimal as a snowman or a pancake is a metaphor. Scientists use metaphors all the time to help us understand what's in our universe.

MORE THAN JUST PLANETS

The more we study our solar system, the more surprises we find. It isn't just empty space out there! When the solar system formed, bits of rock and ice stuck together, creating the planets. But Jupiter and Neptune were so large that their strong gravity made some of those bits crash into one another. Those pieces stayed swirling around the sun in a donut-shaped ring called the Kuiper Belt. It's one of the largest structures in our solar system, full of trillions of pieces of rock, dust and ice called small bodies, or planetesimals, the leftovers from all the crashes.

There are dwarf planets in the Kuiper Belt, too, with irregular orbits and shapes. They don't have enough gravity to clear their paths, so there is a lot of space junk flying around with them.

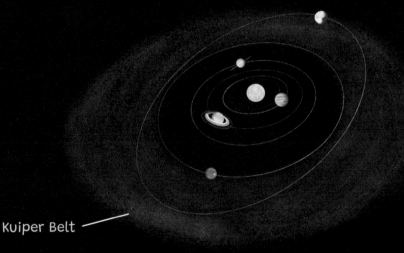

Kuiper Belt

Planetary scientists think there may be another planet in the Kuiper Belt. Planet X, sometimes called Planet 9, is believed to exist because of the way that other objects in the Kuiper Belt move. If Planet X is there, scientists think it is the size of Neptune, but about 20 times farther from the sun. It would take between 10 000 and 20 000 years to complete one orbit around the sun!

The Oldest Snowman

A Butterfly Cinquain for Arrokoth

Two lumps
Stuck together
Like a fat, squashed snowman
Four billion miles away from Earth
Spinning
Red rock
So very old
Might it tell the story
Of how the universe was formed
In time?

ASTEROID ARROKOTH

In 2006, NASA's New Horizons probe left Earth. Even traveling at 16.26 km (10.1 mi.) a second, it took 13 years to get to our solar system's outer edge. In 2019, New Horizons flew by an asteroid in the Kuiper Belt that we now call *Arrokoth*, which means "sky" in Powhatan, a language once spoken by Indigenous peoples in eastern Virginia.

Arrokoth is about 6.5 billion km (4 billion mi.) away from us. It's only 20 km (12 mi.) across, very small in astronomical terms, so we're lucky that the probe found it! Arrokoth is the farthest thing away from Earth that we've photographed up close.

The Kuiper Belt has billions of asteroids, but Arrokoth is special because it's the oldest asteroid we've seen. It was formed at the very beginning of our solar system. Scientists think that by studying Arrokoth, we can find out more about how the universe was formed.

Beyond the Kuiper Belt, there might be a huge outer covering called the Oort cloud. We can't see it, so no one is sure it's there. Even though our spacecraft Voyager 1 is traveling toward the Oort cloud at a million miles a day, it won't get there for three hundred years!

Sun

Oort cloud

Syllabic Cinquains

A cinquain is a poem written using a
specific number of syllables. Like a haiku,
a cinquain tells a story with very few words.
It has only five lines, each with a specific
number of syllables:

FIRST LINE: two syllables
SECOND LINE: four syllables
THIRD LINE: six syllables
FOURTH LINE: eight syllables
FIFTH LINE: two syllables

When you put two cinquains together,
they become a butterfly cinquain — the
shape of Arrokoth, but a lot smaller!

Your Turn
A Hip-Hop Poem for Future Astronomers

Years long past, people thought that our Earth was flat like a bath mat
Travel too far and you'd go splat, over the edge and that'd be that.

Above, they saw a cosmic dome
A closed and covered cozy home
A blue and sparkling astrodome
Below a void without a clone.

But some people asked questions, looked harder
Some people observed, thought longer
Had new ideas that were bolder.
They proved Earth's not flat but a boulder
The sun is a star and much older.

Surprised to discover Earth has a place
A planet like others, it spins through space
Circles the sun at a yearly pace
Rotating each day at its Earthly pace
The human race a jewel in this home base

And that is a truth you cannot erase.

Now it's your turn to learn and discover
Look for new facts you can uncover
Find more things in outer space
See more truths you cannot erase.

BELIEVE THE UNBELIEVABLE, THEN PROVE IT!

Sometimes it's hard for people to believe new things even when they're true. Sometimes people don't want to change their ideas. When the scientist Copernicus (1473–1543) proved that the sun doesn't move, people ignored him. When astronomer Galileo (1564–1642) proved that Earth circles around the sun, and that the sun is the center of a large system of planets, he was put in prison and his books were banned. It's important to remember that sometimes the ideas people think are right might not be. There are always new things to learn. We're discovering new things about the planets, our solar system, our galaxy and our universe every day. By the time you're reading this book, we'll know even more!

Maybe you'll be the one to find a whole new way of understanding our solar system.

Hip-Hop Beats

Hip-hop poetry is written, spoken and sung
more than any other kind of poetry in the world. It is
the poetry of ordinary people talking about their homes
and neighborhoods. It tells the truth, no matter how hard
it is to hear. It's about protest, anger, grief, joy and love.
It's poetry that wants to have a conversation to make a better
world. This poem, "Your Turn," is about the idea that there is
always more to discover about our own "neighborhood."

Sung, spoken or rapped in clubs, beat battles and poetry slams,
hip-hop comes from sound. You have to say it out loud to find the
rhymes and rhythms. The beats emphasize syllables, and the rhymes
are everywhere — at the end and middle of lines or the start and
middle of words. You can feel hip-hop sounds and rhythms
resonate in your whole body.

Try saying this poem to a beat or a soundtrack while
moving around. Play with how you say the words.
Before you know it, you'll be performing with
your own style.

Write Your Own Poem

Writing a poem is very personal. You are the only one who can write your poem. When you write a poem, you say it from your point of view. You think about what the subject of the poem means to you.

Ideas for poems are all around you. When you catch one, think about it for a long time. Look at it, smell it, listen to it, feel it, wrestle with it, throw it up in the air, bounce it on the grass — whatever is needed to make your idea come alive through images, feelings and ideas.

When I wrote this book, I made long lists of information about each planet. I looked at pictures, listened to music (composers have written their own interpretations of the planets) and held rocks in my hands to feel the age of our planet Earth. I stood outside on crisp winter nights, the mist of my breath traveling along the line of the Milky Way, and let the sky fill me with wonder.

To write a poem about a planet, you need to fill yourself with many ideas, images and feelings. Here is something to get you started.

PLANET X

Planet X isn't in this book. Planet X, which is also called Planet 9, is a mysterious, "hypothetical" planet. That means it is an idea based on good information, but no one has proved it exists.

Some astronomers think Planet X exists because there are thousands of planetesimals (page 36) orbiting around something past Neptune. These ETNOs (extreme trans-Neptunian objects) are moving in the same way, influenced by something massive, about Neptune-sized. They are being maneuvered and corralled by something. But if it is there, why have we never seen it?

We discovered Neptune because astronomers and mathematicians could see that Uranus behaved strangely. They thought that there must be another planet. They calculated where it had to be, then they looked there with our most powerful telescopes and found it! Some astronomers think the same thing must be true about Planet X. But if there is a Planet X, it's estimated to be about 90 billion km (56 billion mi.) away from the sun. That's 20 times farther than Neptune! It would be would be *10 billion times* fainter in the sky than Neptune, much fainter than our eyes or best telescopes could see. If there is a Planet X, it would take between 10 000 and 20 000 years to orbit the sun. So the chances of us finding and seeing it are pretty slim!

Astronomer Michael E. Brown says, "If Planet X is there, we'll find it together." He knows that it will take everyone working together to look for this "needle-in-a-haystack" planet. We're building new telescopes to search the sky and maybe one day, we'll find Planet X and add it to our solar system!

WRITE A PLANET X POEM

What does Planet X make you think about? What does it make you feel? What is most interesting to you? Make a list of everything. Now make a list to go with that of words that rhyme, have similar rhythms and make you think of metaphors (images that aren't Planet X, but are somehow similar).

Look at your lists. What words do you really like? Which ones make images in your mind?

Try using the letters P–L–A–N–E–T–X to write an acrostic (page 25). Tell us something special about Planet X on each line.

Try writing a hip-hop poem (page 33) with lots of beats and rhymes inside the lines. Play with different lengths of lines. Let rhymes change in the middle of lines. Play with the sounds. Try starting every line with "If it's there …" Tell people what YOU think about the mystery of Planet X.

Write a prose poem (page 29), with lots of metaphors. You don't need to worry about things rhyming, or even having rhythm. Tell us about Planet X through images, through similar but different things, things you know, things on Earth. Planet X has an elliptical orbit, an egg shape. Where does Planet X take your imagination?

Glossary of Space Terms

atmosphere: the layer of gasses that surround and coat a planet. Every planet's atmosphere is different. Earth's is perfect for life — a blend of nitrogen, oxygen and bits of carbon dioxide and neon. Mars has an atmosphere that is mostly carbon dioxide. Mercury has no atmosphere at all.

density: how much mass there is in an area. A lot of mass in a small area means something is very dense.

dwarf planet: not a small planet, but a scientific term for planet-sized objects that orbit the sun in a noncircular path. There are five official dwarf planets beyond Neptune: Pluto, Ceres, Makemake, Haumea, Eris.

galaxy: a collection of thousands to billions of stars held together by gravity. The galaxy we live in is called the Milky Way, one of an infinite number of galaxies in the universe.

gravity: the force that pulls matter together and that draws things toward the center of a planet, sun or other body. The force of gravity keeps all of the planets in orbit around the sun and keeps all of us on Earth, instead of letting everything fly off into space.

magnetic field: the space around a magnet where the magnetic force is active. Magnetic fields have "poles," ends where the force is positive or negative. On Earth, our north pole and south pole are magnetic fields.

magnetic force: the way that electrically charged particles are pulled toward or away from each other

mass: the amount of matter, or "stuff," that things are made of. You have mass — you usually call it weight. A planet has mass. Even a feather has mass.

matter: the stuff, mostly atoms, that something is made of. The matter you are made of is mostly hydrogen, carbon, nitrogen and oxygen.

planetesimals: small space objects, made of rock, dust or other debris, that formed when the solar system was created and that show us how planets were made

satellite: a moon, planet or machine that orbits a planet

shepherd moon: a satellite that orbits a planet and either makes a path, clearing debris (floating rocks, ice), or pulls debris together into a ring or arc. Jupiter, Saturn, Uranus and Neptune all have shepherd moons.

Sources and Resources

THE PLANETS

Aguilar, David A. *11 Planets: A New View of the Solar System*. National Geographic Society, 2008.

Galat, Joan Marie. *Dot to Dot in the Sky: Stories of the Planets*. Whitecap Books, 2003.

SPACE

Alam, Munazza and Joan Marie Galat. *Absolute Expert: Space*. National Geographic Kids, 2020.

Becker, Helaine and Brendan Mullan. *National Geographic Kids: Everything Space*. National Geographic Kids, 2015.

Berkowitz, Jacob. *Out of This World: The Amazing Search for an Alien Earth*. Kids Can Press, 2009.

Galat, Joan Marie and Gary LaCoste. *Our Universe: Stars*. Scholastic, 2020.

Gater, Will, Angela Rizza and Daniel Long. *The Mysteries of the Universe*. DK and Penguin Random House, 2020.

Morgan, Ben. *Eyewitness Explorer: Night Sky Detective*. DK and Penguin Random House, 2015.

ASTRONAUTS

Hadfield, Chris, Kate Fillion and the Fan Brothers. *The Darkest Dark*. Tundra Books, 2016.

Harris, Jennifer and Louise Pigott. *She Stitched the Stars: A Story of Ellen Harding Baker's Solar System Quilt*. Albert Whitman & Co., 2021.

Krull, Kathleen, Paul Brewer and Frank Morrison. *Starstruck: The Cosmic Journey of Neil deGrasse Tyson*. Crown Books for Young Readers, 2018.

WEBSITES

https://www.britannica.com/science/solar-system/

https://solarsystem.nasa.gov/solar-system/our-solar-system/overview/

https://spaceplace.nasa.gov/

WRITING POETRY

Janeczko, Paul B. (ed.) and Chris Raschka. *A Kick in the Head: An Everyday Guide to Poetic Forms*. Candlewick Press, 2009.

Lesynski, Lori and Michael Martchenko. *I Did It Because: How a Poem Happens*. Annik Press, 2006.

Pretlutsky, Jack. *Pizza, Pigs, and Poetry: How to Write a Poem*. HarperCollins, 2008.

WEBSITES

https://www.kidlit.tv/2017/05/the-kids-are-all-write-how-to-write-a-poem/

https://poetry4kids.com/

https://rhymer.com/

Our Solar System

Uranus

Mars

Jupiter

Neptune

Kuiper Belt

SUN

Mercury

Venus

Earth

Saturn

Pluto and Charon

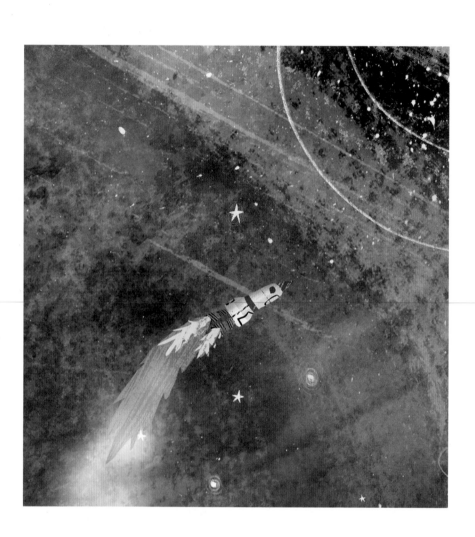